101

FASCINATING FACTS TO KNOW ABOUT

THE HUMAN BODY

Editorial Director: María Jesús Díaz
Designer: Estelle Talavera
Authors: Miriam Baquero, Niko Domínguez
Editor: Ana Doblado
Illustrator: F. Valiente / Susaeta
Translated and edited by Lisa Regan

© SUSAETA EDICIONES, S.A. - Obra colectiva
C/ Campezo, 13 - 28022 Madrid
Tel.: 91 3009100 - 91 3009118
www.susaeta.com

English edition first published 2015 by Brown Watson
The Old Mill, 76 Fleckney Road
Kibworth Beauchamp
Leicestershire LE8 0HG

ISBN: 978-0-7097-2229-8

Printed in Malaysia

101

FASCINATING FACTS TO KNOW ABOUT

THE HUMAN BODY

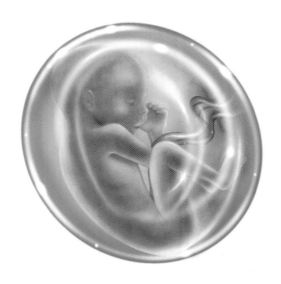

Brown Watson

ENGLAND

Contents

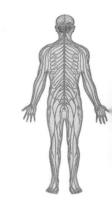

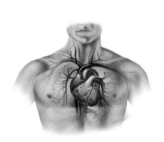

A perfect machine

1 The human body is made up of around 5 billion cells.

These cells form the different organs which, in turn, make up various systems in our body: movement (muscles and bones), respiratory, digestive, excretory, circulatory, endocrine, nervous and reproductive.

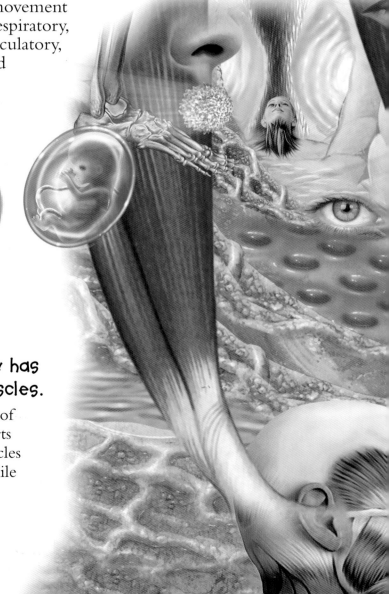

DID YOU KNOW...?
A giraffe's neck contains the same number of bones as a human neck!

2 The human body has more than 600 muscles.

The muscles help many of our organs and body parts work. For example, muscles help us to breathe, to smile and to blink.

3 The body's control centre is the nervous system, which guides and coordinates everything we do.

It is made up of the spinal cord and the nerves, but the most important part is the brain, which controls how our organs work, how we move, and how we feel.

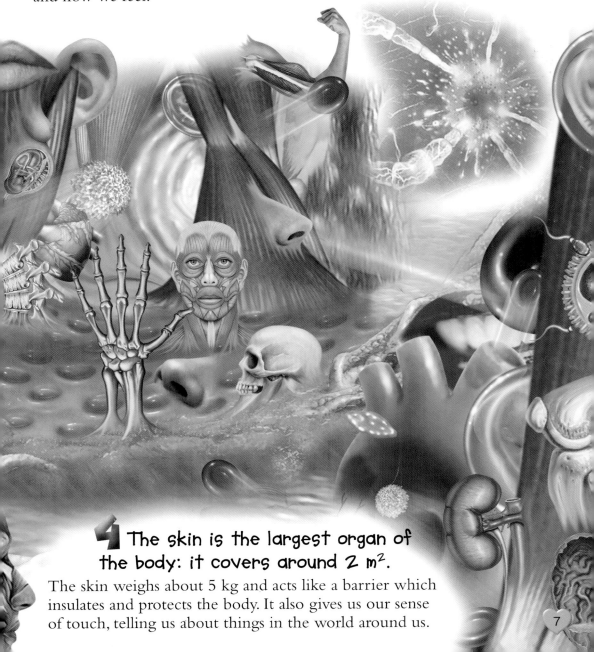

4 The skin is the largest organ of the body: it covers around 2 m².

The skin weighs about 5 kg and acts like a barrier which insulates and protects the body. It also gives us our sense of touch, telling us about things in the world around us.

5 The respiratory system takes in oxygen from the air we breathe and gets rid of carbon dioxide.

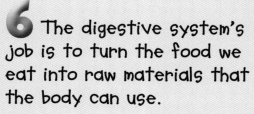

Breathing is one of the many automatic movements that we do. We breathe between 5 and 6 litres of air every minute.

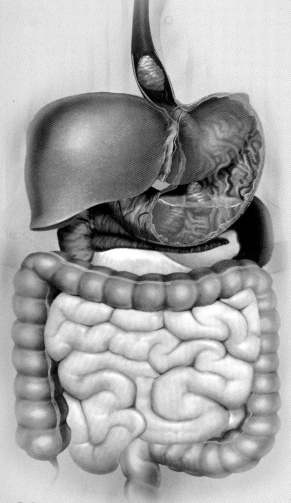

6 The digestive system's job is to turn the food we eat into raw materials that the body can use.

This process can take a whole day, as the food spends between 3 and 5 hours in the stomach and then between 6 and 20 hours more in the large intestine.

7 The excretory system is in charge of getting rid of all the waste products that the body cannot use.

These substances are leftovers; the bits of food that the digestive system cannot absorb, and other substances that are eliminated in different forms. They leave our body as wee, poo and sweat.

8 The circulatory system is like a large network of roads, transporting substances which perform vital jobs to allow our body to work properly.

It carries the oxygen needed by all of our cells, as well as hormones, nutrients and waste products that we need to get rid of. It also controls body temperature, and helps the body to defend itself from infection.

DID YOU KNOW...?

Some drugs can change the colour of urine! These include propofol, which dyes it green, or rifampicin (used to treat tuberculosis), which dyes wee orange.

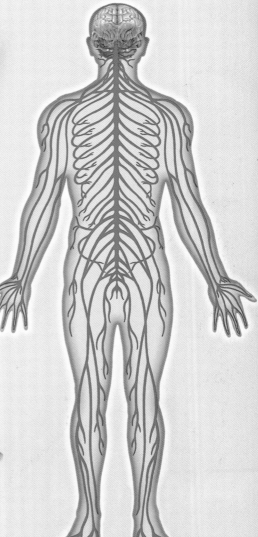

9 The endocrine system is made up of a series of organs and tissues which produce and secrete things called hormones.

These enter directly into the blood stream and control many different bodily functions, such as growth or our moods, as well as many others.

The delicate, complex brain

10 The brain is the most fragile part of the body and, without doubt, the most important.

It is made up of a grey material (on the outside) and a white substance (on the inside). It is split into two parts, or hemispheres, which themselves are made up of areas called lobes.

11 The brain is responsible for our intellectual abilities.

The brain's surface, called the cerebral cortex, is where thinking happens. Scientists disagree about how to measure intelligence, but they do carry out various tests which suggest that 70 out of 100 people have an average Intelligence Quotient (IQ) of between 85 and 115.

12 Human babies, like baby animals, need to sleep much more than adults.

This is because at this stage, the connections in the brain are developing and becoming organised. This is how they reach their adult stage, with the incredible brain power that humans possess.

DID YOU KNOW...?

The average weight of a male adult's brain is around 1,400 g, but this is not linked to how clever the person is: Albert Einstein's brain weighed only 1,230 g!

13 Sleep is vital for life, and thinking and memory will suffer dreadfully if you don't get enough sleep.

During deep sleep the body relaxes, but the brain remains incredibly active. It is thought that we make a permanent record of our memories when we are asleep.

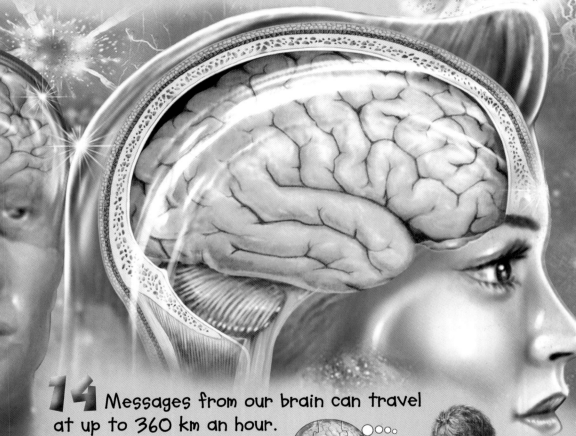

14 Messages from our brain can travel at up to 360 km an hour.

Neurons are the fundamental cells in the nervous system and are in charge of sending nerve impulses at such surprising speeds.

The five senses

15 The magic of the senses

We have five senses: sight, hearing, smell, taste and touch. We hardly realise when they are working, because we are so used to them doing their job. Our senses allow us to interact with other things: seeing, tasting, smelling, touching, listening...they open up the whole world around us!

16 The eye works like a camera

It has two lenses, the cornea and the crystalline lens, which make the images that reach the eye form exactly on the retina. If they form in front or behind it, they will be blurred. The crystalline lens is surrounded by muscles which make it stretch or relax depending whether the objects being viewed are close or far away.

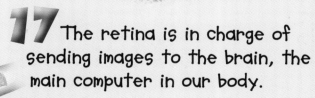

17 The retina is in charge of sending images to the brain, the main computer in our body.

Although it is very thin, the retina has room for ten cell layers! These control what we can see in the daytime and allow us to distinguish different colours, with cells called cones. These cones need enough light to work, which is why we cannot see colours in the dark.

18 Night vision

The cells which control what we can see at night are called rods. They can operate with very little light, although they cannot make out colours. If we move around using only the moonlight, at first we can hardly see anything. However, after only 20 minutes, these rods become 6,000 times more sensitive to the light!

19 Our hearing works because our ears pick up sound waves, which travel towards our eardrum.

The eardrum is a thin membrane, like the skin of a tambourine, which sends vibrations along tiny bones called ossicles. They pass to the inner ear, where the vibrations are turned into an electrical signal to be sent to the brain.

DID YOU KNOW?

If we are subjected to sounds over 100 decibels for a long time, we risk becoming deaf.

20 Be careful on roller coasters!

The ear is linked to the throat by a tube called the Eustacian tube. It helps to balance the pressure inside and outside the ear. This is why, when we go upwards very quickly, our ears feel blocked. The climb has happened too fast for the pressure to be balanced between the outside atmosphere and inside our ear. If you swallow hard, it will open up the Eustacian tube and get rid of the uncomfortable feeling.

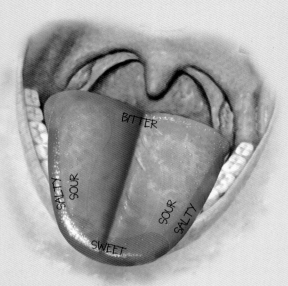

BITTER
SALTY SOUR
SOUR SALTY
SWEET

21 We taste with our tongue

Our tongue is covered with taste buds, which recognise the different parts of what we eat and allow our brain to identify them as flavours: sour, salty, sweet and bitter.

22 Poison alert!

In nature, there are some substances which are poisonous to us. Most of these have a strong bitter taste that puts us off them. This instinct stops us from accidentally eating poisonous plants.

DID YOU KNOW?

There is a new flavour known as *umami* (which means 'delicious taste' in Japanese) and, although we still don't really know how it is produced, it is a flavour which cannot be classified in the same way as before. Strong cheese and some sauces have it.

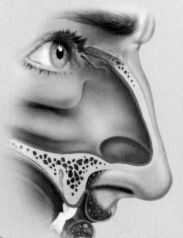

23 Our sense of smell is much less developed than that of many animals.

It is made up of around 100 million cells spread throughout the nose. Our sense of smell can become used to the messages which are sent to the brain. After a while, we stop noticing a smell which seemed very strong just a while before.

24 No taste without smell

As well as picking up scents, the sense of smell allows us to taste our food. You can test this by sucking a mint: you will notice that the flavour is not as strong if you block your nose while you suck it. That is why you can't taste your food as well when you have a cold.

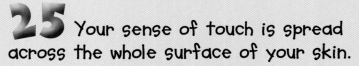

25 Your sense of touch is spread across the whole surface of your skin.

Your skin has special cells for all kinds of sensations, such as vibrations, temperature or the texture of objects. We don't have the same number of these cells on each area of our skin, so some body parts are more sensitive than others. All of them have a limit to their sensitivity so that we can feel pain if it becomes too strong.

The heart and the blood

26 Teamwork!

The heart's job is to pump the blood so that it reaches all of the body. It is divided into two parts: the right receives the blood that is low in oxygen, and sends it to the lungs; the left takes the blood that has collected oxygen from the lungs, and spreads it around the body. The heart moves between 3 and 5 litres of blood every minute! In one year, it moves the same amount of blood as the amount of water in an Olympic swimming pool…more than two million litres!

27 Heartbeats

Each side of the heart consists of an atrium and a ventricle, separated by mitral (left) and tricuspid (right) valves. These valves are 'flaps' which let the blood pass through into the ventricle when the atrium contracts. The blood passes to the major arteries through other valves. When we try to find a person's heartbeat, we are actually listening for the sound of these valves closing.

28 When we exercise, our body needs large amounts of oxygen.

That is why you get that 'out of breath' feeling. The heart contracts faster and stronger, allowing it to go from pumping 5 litres of blood per minute to pumping up to 30 litres!

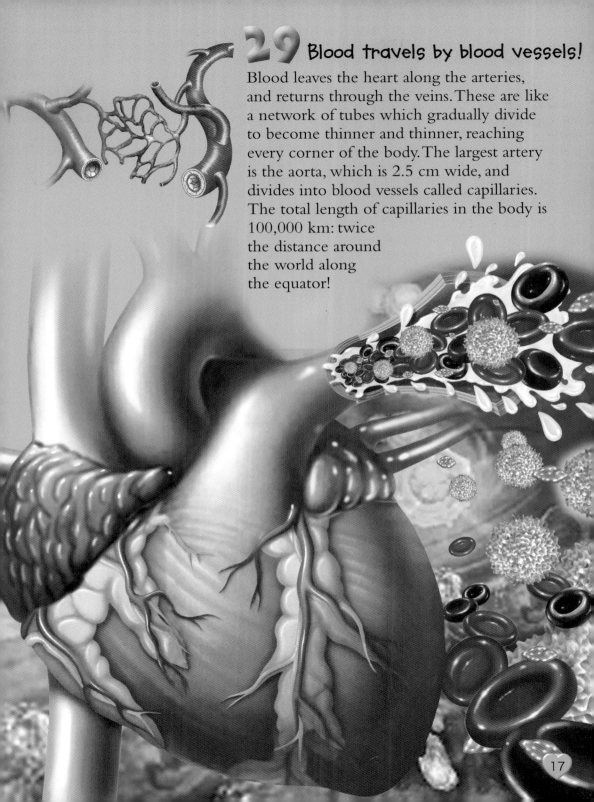

29 Blood travels by blood vessels!

Blood leaves the heart along the arteries, and returns through the veins. These are like a network of tubes which gradually divide to become thinner and thinner, reaching every corner of the body. The largest artery is the aorta, which is 2.5 cm wide, and divides into blood vessels called capillaries. The total length of capillaries in the body is 100,000 km: twice the distance around the world along the equator!

30 What is blood made of?

Blood contains nutrients (such as oxygen or sugar), waste products that need to be discarded (such as carbon dioxide and lactic acid), hormones (which act like messengers inside the body), proteins that do different jobs…and also blood cells: red blood cells, white blood cells and platelets. These blood cells make a substance which is found inside our bones: bone marrow.

Red blood cells

31 We have between 4 and 5 million red blood cells!

These cells are very special because they are formed without a nucleus (usually an important part of any cell). This gives them space to carry more oxygen from the lungs to the body's other organs.

32 White blood cells: guardians in the blood!

There are various types of white blood cell, but all of them have the same job: protecting us from infection. There may be between 4,500 and 10,500 in each mm^3 of blood. The cells have a 'memory': when they overcome an infection, they record how they did it. This allows them to fight it more quickly and effectively the next time, so we may not even become ill. That is how vaccinations work.

White blood cells

33 Platelets to the rescue

If we wound ourselves, we bleed, but only for a short time. The bleeding stops thanks to platelets. These cells work as a team, joining together to fix a broken blood vessel. They help the blood to clot so the blood vessel is able to repair itself.

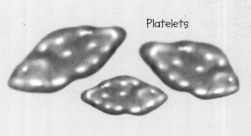

Platelets

34 A heart beats around 3,000 million times in a lifetime.

Luckily, we don't need to instruct our heart to keep beating; it does it by itself because, as well as muscle, the heart has its own electric circuit which automatically keeps a rhythm of around 80 beats per minute.

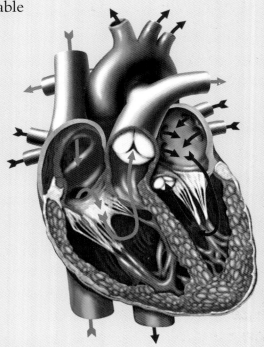

35 Healthy hearts

Professional sportspeople train hard so that their heart can cope with the body's extra requirements during exercise. Their heart pumps more blood with every heartbeat to deliver more oxygen to their muscles. They also have a lower heart rate than non-athletes when they are not doing exercise.

Breathing

36 We breathe because of our lungs

Air reaches the lungs by travelling along an airway made up principally of the trachea and the bronchi. When we breathe properly, taking in air through the nose (not the mouth), the air which reaches the lungs is cleaner and warmer, reducing the risk of catching a cold.

37 When we cough, air comes out at speeds of 140 km/h!

The trachea (for breathing) and the oesophagus (for eating) are both linked to your mouth. When we eat, the trachea closes to stop food entering it, but sometimes this can go wrong. If we accidentally get something other than air in our trachea, we cough to get rid of it.

DID YOU KNOW...?

Charles Osborne, a farmer from the United States, was in the Guinness Book of Records for hiccupping for 68 years! At first he hiccupped at least 40 times a minute, but this slowed to around 20 times a minute in later years.

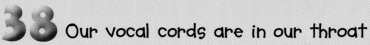

38 Our vocal cords are in our throat

The vocal cords, or folds, which allow us to speak, open and close to let different amounts of air pass through. This is how we make different sounds. When we overstretch our voice, we become hoarse, as our vocal folds become inflamed. This prevents them from closing properly and allows air to escape between them, changing our voice.

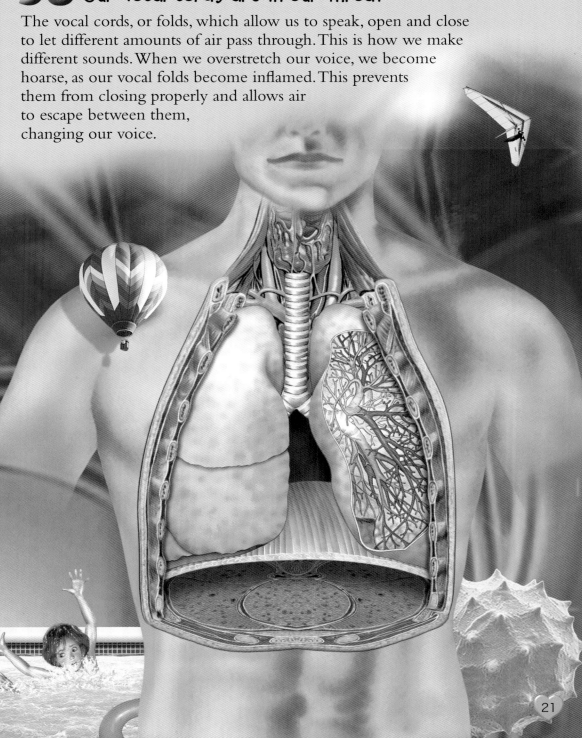

39 Our lungs can hold up to 6 litres of air.

That's not bad for our size, but it doesn't allow us to spend very long underwater. If you want a mammal that can really stay under for a long time, check out the blue whale, which has lungs 3,000 times bigger than ours!

40 480 litres of air every hour!

In reality, we only use a small amount of this capacity during normal breathing: around 0.5 litres. But because we take between 14 and 20 breaths per minute, we can breathe around 480 litres of air per hour!

Alveoli

41 All this air in our lungs has one task: to fill the alveoli.

From here, it passes to the red blood cells, which carry the oxygen around the body. The alveoli are tiny sacs that fill the lungs, making it look like a sponge. If you joined together the surface of all these sacs, they would be the size of a tennis court.

42 When air enters the alveoli, oxygen passes to the blood thanks to the capillaries which surround the alveoli.

When air leaves, the alveoli close, then open again to let more air in. They are like a balloon inflating and deflating over and over again. Your body has an amazing 600 million alveoli altogether!

43 Breathing isn't just about getting oxygen into our blood.

It also gets rid of carbon dioxide, one of our body's waste products. We also, without realising it, lose 350 ml of water vapour every day when we breathe out.

44 Smoking is the biggest cause of premature death in the world.

Every year it kills around 6 million people. It causes up to 29 diseases (of the lungs and heart, for example), including 10 different types of cancer. It is frightening what cigarettes contain: more than 2,000 dangerous substances, including ammonia, arsenic, methane, tar and cyanide.

Digestion

45 Food travels on a long journey through our body while it is being digested.

Digestion turns food, like a sandwich, into much smaller substances that our bodies can use, like protein. Enzymes play a very important part in this process. They magically transform our food into the fuel that we need!

46 It all begins in your mouth...

The journey starts when you chew your food, and it is mixed with saliva. Saliva breaks down your food and makes it easier to swallow. It helps it pass to your stomach without scratching your oesophagus. Saliva also contains enzymes, which begin the process of turning food into carbohydrates.

47 There are three basic food groups: carbohydrates, proteins and fats.

Carbohydrates give us a quick supply of energy, in the form of glucose or sugar. Fats also give us energy, but it is released much more slowly. Proteins are the body's building blocks; they help it to grow and heal. Food also contains tiny amounts of other important substances, such as vitamins and minerals.

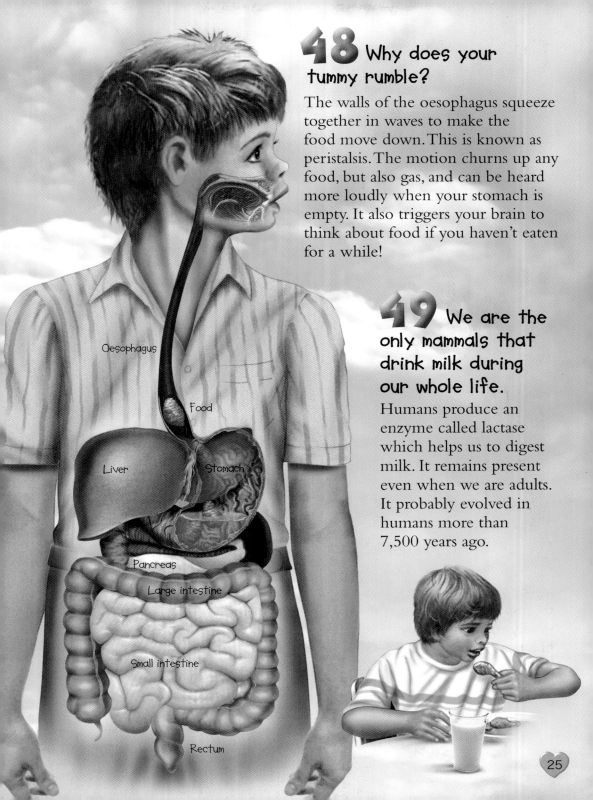

48 Why does your tummy rumble?

The walls of the oesophagus squeeze together in waves to make the food move down. This is known as peristalsis. The motion churns up any food, but also gas, and can be heard more loudly when your stomach is empty. It also triggers your brain to think about food if you haven't eaten for a while!

49 We are the only mammals that drink milk during our whole life.

Humans produce an enzyme called lactase which helps us to digest milk. It remains present even when we are adults. It probably evolved in humans more than 7,500 years ago.

Oesophagus

Food

Liver

Stomach

Pancreas

Large intestine

Small intestine

Rectum

50 The human blender!

When all the food has reached your stomach, the oesophagus closes off so the food can be kept in the stomach and 'blended'. It is crushed together to form a fine paste, ready to be moved into the small intestine. It stays here for between 1 and 4 hours, depending on the type and amount of food you have eaten.

51 Your stomach muscles squeeze tightly to prepare the food for your intestines.

The stomach contracts about three times a minute to stir up the food inside. As well as squeezing, your stomach produces acids and enzymes to help break down the food. It also secretes a type of mucus (a slimy coating) that stops the stomach walls being damaged by the acids.

52 Smaller and smaller

The food that arrives in the small intestine is already well digested. Even so, more enzymes get to work, breaking down the food so that the nutrients in it can be absorbed by the intestine.

DID YOU KNOW...?
A person produces 34,000 litres of saliva during their lifetime.

53 Nutrients for the body

The juices produced by the pancreas and the liver help to digest the food even more. The walls of the intestine absorb the nutrients and pass them to the blood, to feed our organs.

54 If we straightened the small intestine, it would be 6 metres long!

The large intestine is shorter, around 1.5 m. Its job is to remove enough water to turn the food waste into solid matter, ready to pass out of your body as poo.

55 Healthy eating

It is important to avoid eating too much, or choosing too many fatty foods. A balanced diet is vital to help you grow properly. You should also exercise regularly so that your body uses up its food supplies instead of storing them as fat. People who are overweight are more likely to suffer from cardiovascular diseases and other health problems.

The muscles

56 Outside and in

Muscles are needed to move our body, and make up the largest part of our bodyweight (40%). We usually think of them working together to make us move around, operating our arms and legs. But we also have muscles in our internal organs – such as the heart, to pump the blood, and the oesophagus, to move our food into our stomach.

57 There are two basic muscle types: striated and smooth.

Striated muscles are also called voluntary muscles. We make conscious movements with them. Smooth (involuntary) muscle contracts without us realising, for example the muscle that forms the stomach wall.

58 Going to extremes

The longest muscle in the human body is the sartorius, which runs down the thigh from the pelvis to the knee. The shortest is the stirrup, which measures 1.26 mm and is inside the ear.

Muscle

59 Muscles are joined to the bones by powerful fibres called tendons.

Muscles are made to contract by impulses carried along nerves. In fact, if a muscle does not receive these impulses, it will not move, and will eventually waste away and become useless.

DID YOU KNOW...?

The strongest muscle is in your head and is called the masseter muscle. It helps you to bite, chew and clench your jaw, and can create a pressure of 80 kg per cm^2.

Myofibril

Protein chain

Muscle cells

60 Pull, not push

Muscles work by contracting and pulling on the body part they are attached to. They cannot push, so they work in opposing pairs. When one muscle contracts, the other relaxes, and then vice versa to undo the action.

61 Muscle messages

Your facial muscles allow you to blink, wink, smile, frown, even whistle if you're able! The muscles which control blinking are the fastest in the body: we can open and close our eyelids up to five times a second!

62 Mighty mouth

The most powerful muscle, for its size, is the tongue – although it isn't actually just one muscle. It is made up of separate muscles that work as a team. Some of these attach the tongue to the mouth and move it around. Other muscles within the tongue alter its shape and size.

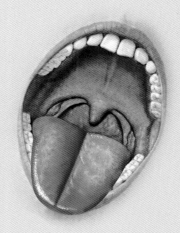

63 Many muscles

There are over 640 muscles in the human body, of varying sizes and formations. It's hard to believe how many muscles it takes to perform a simple action, like walking: no less than 200! The face has around 43 muscles, although some people have more, and other people have less than that!

64 Humans and other primates have evolved differently from most creatures, thanks to one very important muscle.

It is a small, triangular muscle in the hand which moves our thumb. It lets us pinch together the thumb and index finger to grasp things.

Bones: the tough guys!

65 **The skeleton is the support for our whole body.**

Our bones, together with our muscles, move us around. The place where two bones meet is called a joint. Bones also protect our fragile internal organs: the skull protects the brain, the spine or backbone protects the spinal cord, the ribs protect the lungs and heart, and so on.

66 **We have 206 bones altogether...**

...although we are born with more. A baby's bones do not make up its final skeleton: as it matures some of the bones fuse together. They harden and change into adult bones.

Without a helmet

With a helmet

Other fractures are cleaner and only the bone is broken.

The inside of a bone has its own blood and circulation, and is a living organ.

If a bone is fractured, the blood vessels break.

Blood covers the fracture and forms a clot.

The clot hardens and forms new bone.

Gradually, it returns to how it was before the break..

If you break your arm or leg a long way from a hospital, it is best to put the limb in a splint.

In some fractures, the bone can break through the skin.

67 There are three main types of bone.

They are long, short and plate (flat). Long bones are made up of a middle section, the diaphysis, and two rounded end sections, the epiphyses. In between there is cartilage. This area of soft tissue allows the bones to grow longer until the body is fully grown, when the cartilage disappears.

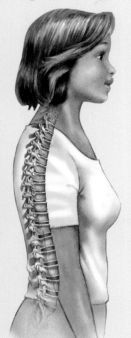

68 Bones are made of a compact part and a spongy part.

The outer part of a bone is compact bone which forms a smooth, continuous surface. Spongy bone is found inside some bones. It is lighter and softer than compact bone, and is like a honeycomb with spaces inside it. The spaces are often filled with bone marrow, which makes new blood cells.

X-rays give us a clear image of the bones.

69 Soft but tough

Although spongy bone may seem weaker, in reality it is difficult to break. The layers that make up the bone can move and shift with pressure, like a well-made building in an earthquake. A small piece of bone is stronger than a piece of cement of the same size.

70 The skull has eight bones and the face has fourteen.

The bones in the skull are locked together by fibres called sutures. This gives extra protection to the brain. These sutures are not formed in newborn babies, making their skull much more flexible. It allows the skull bones to shift during childbirth, making it easier for the baby to fit through the birth canal.

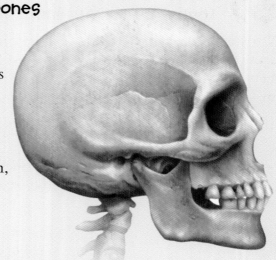

71 Mineralisation

This process is the final flourish, to give us our amazing bones. The bones get two vital minerals – calcium and phosphorous – making the bones even stronger.

72 Our teeth have evolved to handle the different foods we eat.

We have 32 teeth: 8 incisors (for cutting), 4 canines (for tearing), 8 premolars and 12 molars (for chewing). We don't need as many teeth, nor such big, sharp ones, as some other animals. The great white shark, for example, can have 3,000 teeth lined up in many rows!

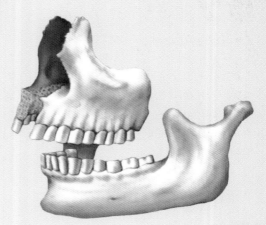

The liver and the kidneys

73 These organs are our body's filters, to get rid of toxins in the blood.

Where do these toxins come from? Sometimes they are produced naturally by the things we eat. Some of them come from chemicals or drugs. Our liver and kidneys do a great job of getting rid of things we don't need.

74 Too much alcohol can damage your liver.

Some substances cannot be eliminated by the liver, but instead are broken down to become less dangerous, or to allow the kidneys to handle them. This purifying process takes its toll on the liver. Too much alcohol makes it work extra hard and, over time, can be dangerous.

DID YOU KNOW...?

During the first few weeks of pregnancy, it is the fetus's liver that produces blood cells.

Alcohol abuse can cause cirrhosis of the liver.

36

75 The liver is the body's factory!

As well as cleaning your blood, the liver is busy doing other jobs. It produces bile, which is important for digestion. It also stores sugar, in the form of glycogen, in case you need extra energy. The liver is the largest internal organ, and weighs 1.5 kg.

Liver

76 The kidneys: vital organs!

If your body was a boat caught in a storm, your kidneys would be the last to abandon ship! They are just as important as your other organs, but often undervalued. Your kidneys can adapt to poor conditions, but are constantly doing their best to keep the body healthy and in good working order.

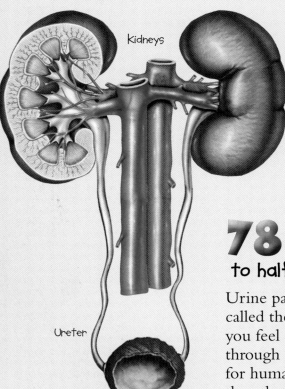

Kidneys

Ureter

Bladder

77 A kidney's job

The kidneys are complex. Although their main job is to produce urine, it isn't a simple task. They also, among other things, make hormones and vitamins, control your blood pressure, and balance fluid levels in your body.

78 The bladder can contain up to half a litre of urine!

Urine passes to the bladder through tubes called the ureters, and then is stored until you feel the need to pee. It leaves your body through the urethra. Urine is a waste product for humans, but for some animals it is more than that. They use it as a scent to mark their territory and pass messages to other members

79 Your kidneys have to filter out all of the bad things in your blood...

... without getting rid of important proteins and minerals. Blood flows in and out of the kidneys, and the liquid part (called plasma) is filtered. The kidneys work hard: in just one day they filter 180 litres of plasma! Your body contains 3 litres of plasma, which passes through the kidneys 60 times every day.

80 Not all the filtered liquid is turned to urine.

As you can imagine, if we peed 180 litres each day, we would soon be dehydrated! After being filtered, the plasma travels along tubes which absorb most of the water, and the filtered substances which are still needed are returned to the blood. That means urine contains only the things that we need to get rid of.

81 Thank goodness we have two kidneys!

If one of them is damaged, we can survive with just the other one. In fact, in a few rare cases, some people are born with just one kidney! However, if both kidneys fail, a dialysis machine is needed to do their job. The machine removes waste products, controls blood pressure, and keeps a safe level of chemicals in the blood, just like healthy kidneys would do.

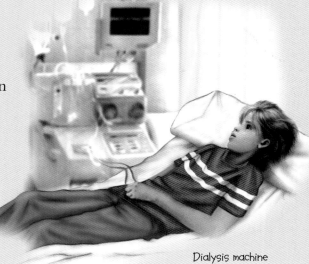

Dialysis machine

DID YOU KNOW...?

The first kidney transplant between living patients took place in 1954. The donor and patient were identical twins, to stop the organ being rejected.

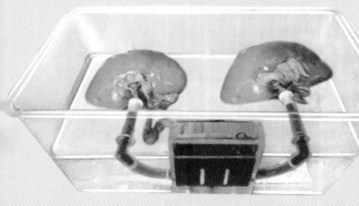

Kidneys ready for a transplant

The wonder of life

82 Bringing a new life into the world begins with the joining of two cells: an egg cell (ovum) and a sperm cell.

These cells are special because each contains half of the chromosomes of a body's cells. When they join, they bring together the 46 chromosomes that contain the genetic instructions (the genome) to make a new human, combining information from both parents.

83 A woman's body has cycles that allow her to reproduce.

A female has ovaries which are in charge of producing the ovum, or egg. One egg is released around every 28 days. The egg travels down the Fallopian tubes to the uterus where it may be fertilised. If this happens, it will be the beginning of a new life!

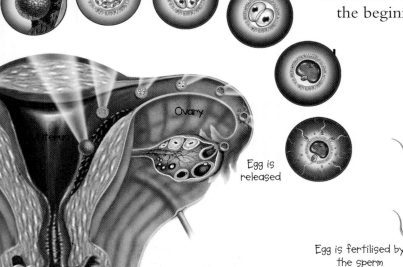

Uterus

Ovary

Egg is released

Egg is fertilised by the sperm

84 The ovaries get a woman's body ready to be pregnant.

They produce oestrogen and progesterone, which are hormones that control the mother's development during pregnancy, and prepare her body for childbirth and bringing up a baby.

85 A precious cargo

A woman, when she is born, has around a million eggs, which will steadily die as she gets older. By the age of 12, this number will have reduced to about 300,000, and only around 400 of them will be ovulated during the woman's lifetime.

86 Sperm are produced in a man's testicles.

Unlike a woman, a man is not born with a particular number of sperm cells, but begin to produce them after they go through puberty. This process carries on until they are 80 or 90 years old, during which time they will produce millions and millions of these cells.

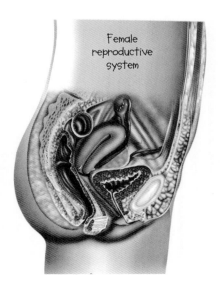

Female reproductive system

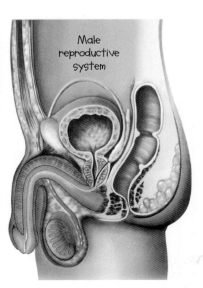

Male reproductive system

87 From hundreds of millions of sperm cells, only one actually fertilises the egg!

The testicles produce sperm and testosterone, the male sex hormone, and release around 300 million sperm in every ejaculation. When one sperm cell reaches the egg, it uses chemicals to create a barrier, stopping other sperm from entering. At this point, the sperm loses its tadpole-like tail.

88 The sperm's treasure hunt for the egg can last up to a week.

The sperm can live in the woman's body for between two and seven days, and can find its way to fertilise the egg at any time.

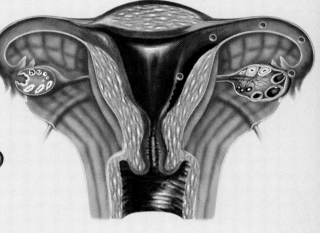

89 A fertilised egg

Once the egg is fertilised, it is called a zygote. It begins to divide, first into two cells, then into four, then eight, and so on. It takes just four days for the first two cells to become more than thirty cells!

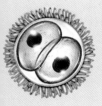    

90 A three-day journey through the Fallopian tubes

The newly fertilised egg has one aim: to get to the uterus, where it implants itself in the walls to spend the next nine months developing. During this journey, it continues to grow, and after six days the two original cells have become an embryo.
A new life is on its way.

91 Twins and triplets...

Sometimes, the fertilised egg splits into two, and becomes identical twins. In this case, both babies will be the same gender. At other times, two eggs may be fertilised at the same time, and both develop, leading to non-identical twins. They share some genetic instructions, so look as similar as any other brother or sister would do. If three eggs are fertilised, triplets will be born.

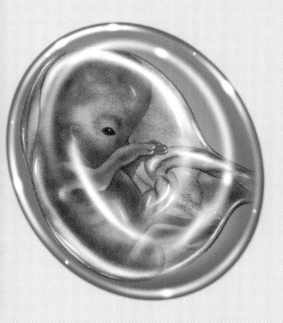

92 The moment in which we are the most top-heavy!

Once the egg is lodged in the uterus, around 14 days after fertilisation, it begins to develop into the embryo and placenta. From now until the twelfth week of pregnancy the various organs grow and develop. The third trimester is when we are most top-heavy: the head is half the total body length!

93 The fetus puts on lots of weight in the last trimester: it grows from 1 kg to more than 3 kg.

Its internal organs also mature, ready to face life on the outside. The lungs are the most important of these organs.

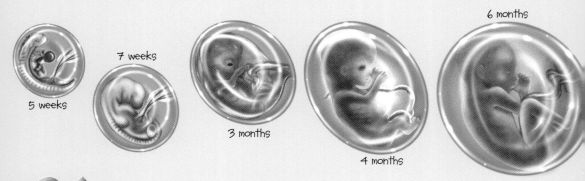

5 weeks

7 weeks

3 months

4 months

6 months

94 The fetus develops while floating in a liquid called amniotic fluid.

This bag of fluid helps to protect the fetus inside its mother's uterus. The amount changes as the fetus swallows some liquid, or releases it as urine. When a woman goes into labour, it is often said that her 'waters have broken'. This means that the fetus has broken the bag which surrounds it, letting the liquid out.

95 A mystery

One thing which has puzzled scientists is why the baby is not rejected by the mother's immune system. Technically, it is a foreign body within the mother, which her body might try to get rid of. However, for various reasons which are still being studied, the rejection doesn't happen, and the pregnancy continues with the baby developing inside.

96 Ready for the world that's waiting.

During childbirth, the uterus contracts and the neck of the uterus opens up to allow the baby to make its way to the outside world. It isn't easy; the baby must turn the right way to allow it to come out properly, so that its head is facing downwards.

9 months, at the moment of childbirth

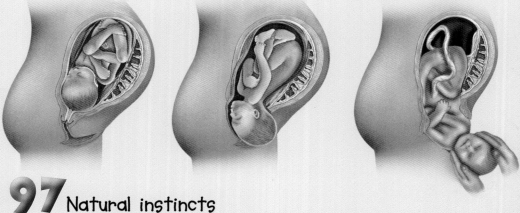

97 Natural instincts

Thanks to advances in medicine, many problems during childbirth can now be solved with surgery. The main concern is that the baby doesn't suffer – that it has enough oxygen, and that a doctor is there to check its wellbeing as soon as it enters the outside world from its cosy home. A newborn will instinctively search for its mother's breast, looking for food.

A guide for life

98 Eat and drink healthily.

Drink between 1.5 and 2 litres of water every day, especially in summer, when the heat can make us lose much more liquid which can lead to serious problems. Eat a balanced, varied diet, with foods from each of the different groups: dairy, meat, eggs, fish, fruit and vegetables, cereals, and small amounts of sugars and fats. Take care not to include too much of these last two in your diet, or your weight will increase and your health will suffer.

99 Wash your hands!

Hygiene is vital to prevent infection. It is especially important to keep our hands clean, as we use them in nearly everything we do. Be very careful with your eyes, because although they have their own cleaning system (tears) you should not touch them with dirty hands.

100 Sleep for 9 to 10 hours.

Sleep is vital to restore the energy that you have used. It is also important for your health, your moods and for how well you can think. Stay in tune with your body clock: day and night are linked with changes in the body's hormone levels and brain activity.

Keep your surroundings clean, as well as your body!

101 Exercise, play sport, and breathe properly.

Try to live an active life, playing the sports you like the most, taking the stairs instead of the lift, and walking as much as possible. Physical activity is extremely important for a healthy life. Also, try to breathe through your nose! It is easy to breathe through your mouth, especially during exercise, to try to take in larger quantities of air. However, it is a mistake, as air breathed through the nose is better for us. It passes through the nasal filters, and is warmed on its journey, both of which help to reduce our chances of infection.

Take care of your back, as your spine is very vulnerable. Be careful how you sit and stand, walk and sleep, as your posture makes a big difference to your spinal health.

Index